U0834042

USING THIS BOOK

*Children learn to read by **reading**, but they need help to begin with.*

When you have read the story on the left-hand pages aloud to the child, go back to the beginning of the book and look at the pictures together.

Encourage children to read the sentences under the pictures. If they don't know a word, give them a chance to 'guess' what it is from the illustrations, before telling them.

There are more suggestions for helping children to learn to read in the *Parent/Teacher* booklet.

British Library Cataloguing in Publication Data
McCullagh, Sheila K.
    Danger! Dragon. —(Puddle Lane. Stage 2; v.9)
    1. Readers—1950-
    I. Title   II. Davis, Jon   III. Series
    428.6   PE1119
    ISBN 0-7214-0932-6

First edition

Published by Ladybird Books Ltd Loughborough Leicestershire UK
Ladybird Books Inc Lewiston Maine 04240 USA

Printed in England

Danger!
Dragon!

written by SHEILA McCULLAGH
illustrated by JON DAVIS

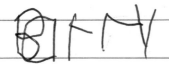

This book belongs to:

BIMY

Ladybird Books

Jeremy Mouse was talking to
Grandmother Mouse, in the big hole
under the hollow tree
in the Magician's garden.
"It's quite safe in the garden,"
he said. "The dragon's not there.
He is chained up to a wall
down the lane. He can't hurt us."
"Don't be too sure of that!"
said Grandmother Mouse.
"If you go into the garden,
look out for dragons!"
"I will," said Jeremy.

Grandmother Mouse said,
"Look out for dragons."

Jeremy was right. The little dragon
was in Mr Puffle's garden.
Mr Puffle had chained him
up to a wall.
But the little dragon was doing his best
to get free.
He twisted his head around,
and breathed out fire
on a link in the chain.
The link grew longer and thinner.
The little dragon jerked his head –
and the chain snapped!
The little dragon was free.

The little dragon was free.

He flew up out of the garden,
and over the roof of the house.
He flew down Puddle Lane.
He looked in at a window.
He saw Miss Baker.
She was baking some cakes.
Sarah and Gita were with her.
The dragon flew in.
He flew on to the table.
He didn't breathe fire, and
he didn't breathe smoke.
He looked at Miss Baker, and
he wept two dragon tears.

The dragon flew in.
He flew on to the table.
He looked at Miss Baker.

Miss Baker was very kind-hearted.
"You poor little thing!" she said.
"Your collar is **much** too tight.
That must be why you are weeping.
Come here, and I'll take it off."
"Don't take it off!" cried Sarah.
"Don't take it off!" cried Gita.
"It's a dragon – a little dragon."
"Nonsense," said Miss Baker.
"There aren't any dragons."
And she took off the dragon's collar.

"Don't take it off,"
cried Sarah.
"Don't take it off,"
cried Gita.
"It's a dragon —
a little dragon."

The dragon leapt up, into the air.
He laughed a dragon laugh.
He breathed out fire, and
he breathed out smoke.
He flew down on to the table.
He breathed over Miss Baker's cakes —
and all in a moment,
the cakes were burnt up.
The little dragon laughed again.
He flew out of the window,
and off into Puddle Lane.

The little dragon flew down
on to the table.

Captain Kay was in Puddle Lane.
Davy was with him.
Captain Kay was very old.
He walked with a stick.
He was going to market, and
Davy was going with him,
to carry his basket.

Captain Kay
was in Puddle Lane.
Davy was with him.

The little dragon saw Captain Kay.
"I'll burn off his whiskers!"
cried the little dragon.
"I don't like whiskers.
The Magician has whiskers."
And he flew straight
at Captain Kay.

The little dragon
saw Captain Kay.
He flew at Captain Kay.

Davy saw the dragon.
He swung the basket,
and hit the little dragon
as the dragon flew by.
He knocked the dragon sideways.
The dragon swung around in the air.
He seized Captain Kay's hat
in his claws, and flew away with it.
"It's a dragon!" cried Captain Kay.
"It's a little dragon.
I never saw a dragon before."

"It's a dragon!"
cried Captain Kay.
"It's a little dragon!"

19

The little dragon was very angry.
He was very hungry, too.
He remembered the mice,
who lived in the hollow tree
in the Magician's garden.
He dropped Captain Kay's hat
in Puddle Lane.
He flew up the lane,
and over the gates
into the Magician's garden.

The little dragon flew
up the lane.
He flew over the gates,
and into the garden.

The Gruffle was in the Magician's garden.
The Gruffle was a monster.
He was very gruff and grumpy.
He could vanish when he wanted to,
but he often left his ears showing.
He was standing behind
one of the bushes.

The Gruffle was in
the Magician's garden.

The little dragon saw two red ears,
sticking up in the air,
over the top of a bush.
The little dragon didn't know
what they were, but he thought
that they might be good to eat.
He was very hungry.
He flew at the ears,
and bit one.

The little dragon saw
two red ears.
He flew at the ears,
and bit one.

There was a roar like thunder,
and there was the Gruffle!
He was very, very angry.
He breathed out fire, and
he breathed out smoke.

There was the Gruffle!

The Gruffle was so big, that
the little dragon was frightened.
He flew away
as fast as he could.
He flew up into the air.
He flew by the Magician's window,
and on to the roof of the house.

The little dragon flew away
as fast as he could.
He flew
by the Magician's window.

The Magician saw him.
The Magician had been making
dragon-magic,
in case the little dragon came back.
When he saw the little dragon,
the Magician picked up
a red ball from his table.
He went back to the open window.

The Magician saw the dragon.
He picked up a red ball
from his table.
He went to the window.

The little dragon was still on the roof.
He looked down into the garden.
The Gruffle had vanished.
Jeremy Mouse came out of his hole.
He looked all around him,
but he didn't look up,
so he didn't see the dragon.
Jeremy Mouse sat down
on a rock.

The little dragon looked
down into the garden.
Jeremy Mouse came out
of his hole.
He sat down on a rock.

The little dragon flew down
from the roof.
He flew straight at Jeremy Mouse.
He breathed out fire, and
he breathed out smoke,
and he flew down as straight
as an arrow.
Jeremy looked up, and saw
the little dragon.
But he was so frightened
that he couldn't move.

The little dragon flew down
from the roof.
Jeremy looked up, and
saw the dragon.

The Magician leaned out of the window.
He threw down the magic ball.
The magic ball shone like red fire.
It broke over the dragon's head.
A cloud of red sparks
rained down on the little dragon.

The magic ball broke over
the little dragon.

As soon as the red sparks
touched him, the little dragon
turned into stone.
He fell down to the ground in the garden.
Jeremy Mouse turned round,
and ran back down the hole
under the hollow tree.

The dragon fell down.
Jeremy Mouse ran back
down the hole
under the tree.

The Magician went down
to the garden.
He picked up the dragon, and
took him back to his room.
He put the dragon on a shelf.
"You stay there," said the Magician.
"You promised not to eat anyone
who lived in the garden, and
you were going to break your promise.
There's one thing you must remember:
You should **always** keep promises.
And you should never, never, NEVER
break a promise you have made
to a magician!"

''Never, never, NEVER
break a promise,''
said the Magician.

Notes for the parent/teacher

When you have read the story, go back to the beginning. Look at each picture and talk about it, pointing to the caption below, and reading it aloud yourself.

Run your finger along under the words as you read, so that the child learns that reading goes from left to right. (You needn't say this in so many words. Children learn many useful things about reading by just reading with you, and it is often better to let them learn by experience, rather than by explanation.) When you next go through the book, encourage the child to read the words and sentences under the illustrations.

Don't rush in with the word before she* has time to think, but don't leave her struggling for too long. Always encourage her to feel that she is reading successfully, praising her when she does well, and avoiding criticism.

Now turn back to the beginning, and print the child's name in the space on the title page, using ordinary, not capital letters. Let her watch you print it: this is another useful experience.

*Children enjoy hearing the same story many times. Read this one as often as the child likes hearing it. The more opportunities she has of looking at the illustrations and **reading** the captions with you, the more she will come to recognise the words. Don't worry if she **remembers** rather than **reads** the captions. This is a normal stage in learning.*

If you have a number of books, let her choose which story she would like to have again.

**Footnote:* In order to avoid the continual "he or she", "him or her", the child is referred to in this book as "she". However, the stories are equally appropriate to boys and girls.

Have you read the other stories about the little dragon?

Stage 2

from The dragon's egg

from Never trust dragons